"Maxwell I. Gold's *Songs of Enough* is an odyssey of the damned into the haunting landscapes of introspection, dystopian visions, and profound existential inquiry. Gold masterfully weaves together rich and evocative imagery to conjure a world both ethereal and viscerally real. Through cycles of lyrical intensity, the collection confronts the reader with stark reflections on technology, identity, and the nature of consciousness itself. These poems echo with urgency and poetic beauty that linger well beyond their reading, marking Gold as a compelling and necessary voice in contemporary poetry."—Angela Yuriko Smith, award-winning author and publisher of *Space and Time*

"A metaphysical labyrinth that is as much about human frailty as it is about the vast, uncaring machinery of the universe. A symphony of sorrow and beauty."—Tim Waggoner, four-time Bram Stoker Award winner

"Weaving dark themes, fluid lyricism, and a cosmic, dreamlike, and often macabre mythos, *Songs of Enough: An Inferno All My Own* is an epic hallucinatory poetry collection that stands alongside the great works of Dante."—Pedro Iniguez, Bram Stoker Award-nominated author of *Mexicans on the Moon: Speculative Poetry from a Possible Future*

"Like a darker, more eschatological Ginsberg, Maxwell Ian Gold weaves a terrifying tapestry of the deeply personal and the contemporary political, the cosmic and the cyber and the physical. The language is frank and blackly beautiful, the themes horrific, but grounded in *the human* in a time when it seems that our very humanity is under assault."—Matthew Bartlett

Songs of Enough

Songs of Enough

An Inferno All My Own

Maxwell I. Gold

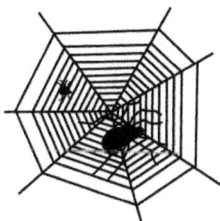

Hippocampus Press

New York

Published by Hippocampus Press
P.O. Box 641, New York, NY 10156
www.hippocampuspress.com

Cover and interior artwork by Daniel V. Sauer, incorporating
vintage works by Gustave Doré, copyright © 2025 by Daniel V. Sauer,
dansauerdesign.com
Hippocampus Press logo designed by Anastasia Damianakos.

First Edition
1 3 5 7 9 8 6 4 2

ISBN 978-1-61498-479-5

Contents

Proem

Enough is enough, the song that played ceaselessly the music of spirit-bile again and over with deathful charm. Trumpeting to the cosmic drum beats, those new gods, the Cyber Gods birthed from senseless *thems* and *others,* things like a pleasurable burst of stars and strokes; they were the beginning of humanity's unreal, unraveling spiral towards that which remained, again, a broken city of skulls, displaced and the hunger and inclinations, continued, which were never enough. When enough was enough and songs sought to continue their tempo like awful tides in my heart, the terrible chorus of what-was-to-come, a vision—over and over—a cycle unbroken caught in some infinite cursed loop.

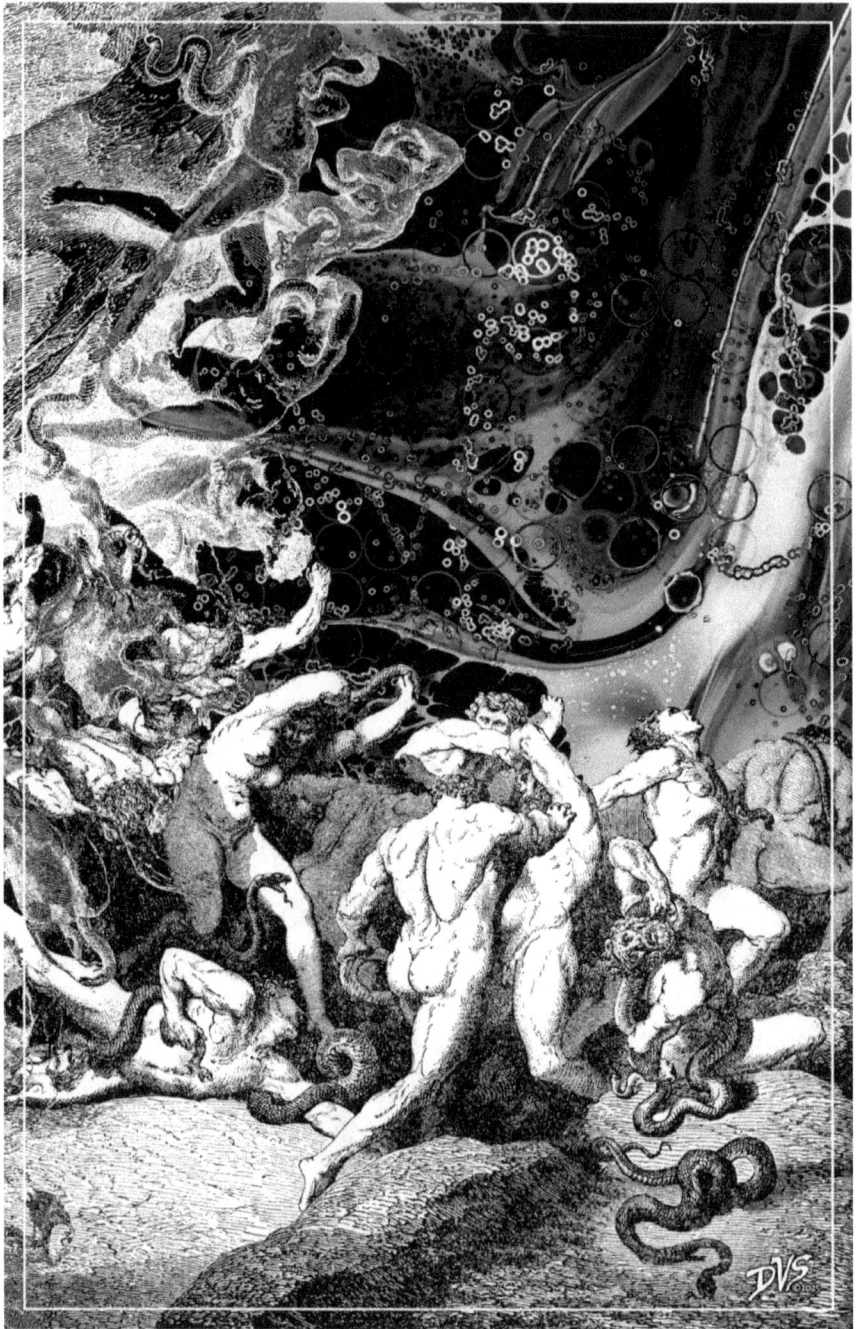

Songs of Enough

When the skies curdle into ash and sand the water of the gods dried up and useless, or the mountains crumbled into mud and bile;

When the cities of plastic races coalesced into a mass of prostrated civilizations, their bodies piled over one another, higher and higher until replaced and beheaded by the blades of burgeoning progress;

When cyber fascitoids stormed the Old Citadel of Thought, tossing the corpses of liberalism into black, burning pits filled with misinformed monsters, ready to feed on the flesh of never-again;

When the stars themselves were unable to handle the presence of Tomorrow, collapsing unto themselves in so much stupendous death;

When there was no tomorrow and the subjective was as fickle as dreams like the strands of hair, so platitudinous and dull, twirled by the fingers of gods;

When the darkness and reason of life mired in shadow and ink, pressed beneath the jeering laughter of crimson faces and nothing seems to make any sense;

When outside the gates of Someday, I stood othered and broken, never able to be *one of them;*

When the ungrateful children of a bastardized Yesterday continued to see me as a trinket whose value was manipulatable, chimeric, and replaceable, they tossed me out for the next best thing;

When flaws of capital were so endless, seemingly flush with fatty excess there was no end to the richness of the horrid opulence that was humanity;

When too late, too late they refused to look up from the bosoms of cyber nursemaids who showered them in baths of pixilated milk and virtualized tube-machines, never waning from that which was so sleek and unreal;

When the mind was deranged, devolved into something plastic and new, and flesh decayed leaving room for the metal and monster so nothing remained;

When I screamed towards the skies as I saw the ballots burn for the sake of the Twentieth Day and coarse shouts scarred my mind, no, not again;

When being sick and tired finally drained the hatred of a billion dead stars, whose awful weight threatened to crush me;

When the night became something like legend, a bulwark of my nightmares pressed deep inside the rhizomatic tunnels carved throughout my skull;

When the clouds were gone, the sun swallowed by some quasar's hunger;
Yesterday,
On the tube machines,
          more black dreams
               Appeared like crystalized hope,

                                        through rusty

hallucinations.

When no longer the dreams of my yesterday were wrapped in treasonous cycles of what-if or never-again;

First Cycle

When the spirit-bile dried up leaving dream-scars and blood-memories in my mind while happily, I closed the doors;

When the skies above were cleansed of ash and soot, or the mountains rebuilt from the same mud and bile;

When the cities of plastic men found yet another ridiculous contrivance to feed their cyber-lust;

When there were no more lights in the night sky, or stars to guide the wandering souls, pixelated or real;

When hallucinations no longer beguiled the weak minds of flesh-things, but were swallowed, byte by byte;

When the ghosts of phantom-machines were resurrected as zombified gods to consume the world of Someday, and I laughed, laughed so damn much;

When death itself was no longer useful, the dead gods of before-yesterday, like some outdated program, floppy disks, corroded and unheard-of;

When diseases found their new meaning in the metal and mind, our bodies irrelevant, useless lights, empty vessels;

When reason was replaced by algorithms, dictated by the new calculous in an expanding, unforgiving universe without care for dogma or pantheons;

When I had finally had enough of these useless words, progress stamping into the mud under its boots, never-again and crimson pus;

When the Old Gates lay rusted and forgotten beneath the overgrown ruins of the Colonial City, and the White Hoods dead;

When these thoughts were thoughts no more, but action and respect until the fatty excess was burnt to the bone;

When the mind no longer evolved, but sat alone, fat and happy while the rest of us were transmogrified and deranged into something, something even worse and nothing remained of what I knew to be myself or the world I knew;

When the lights went out like dying whispers of a aged and petty race, whose reconciliations were pitiful reminders as if shadows etched into stone;

When mass extinction became nothing but a strange concept, or fantasy, and the Plastics never stopped. Billions, trillions of them. Two, three, seven? How many it didn't really matter. Or galaxies themselves consumed by Entropy's endless inclinations;

When sufficiency was equalized through cruel cosmic balance, or it continued through birth, death, light, or dark;

When the questions never stopped, leaving them unanswered like some ruined temple in the deserts of my mind, thick with cruddy brain-matter and bile; more and more they continued;

When the cycles never stopped, or started and all that mattered were the meaningless, empty shells;

When enough was never enough and I found myself wandering ever so lonely into the deepest parts of my memory begging, no pleading for,

When this reprise dared to continue to play on in my mind, over and over, enough never being enough;

When I couldn't see an end to the madness bulging from the scorched horizons unraveling in spiral episodes of rage;

When I prayed I might finally see sweet oblivion;

When the hunger and inclinations, continued, which were never enough, I might finally remember there something worth remembering . . .
. . . Yesterday,
through tube machines,
      inside black dreams

                appeared like crystalized hope,
                  through rusty, deceitful
       hallucinations.

DVS ©2021

Absent Storms

Words like *petit mal, epileptic, broken, unused* were strange signifiers that honestly made me feel as if I was some pale, fleshy alien that never really belonged on this planet. Perhaps the same creatures I saw in my head, tempests that sabotaged my ability to think, to scream, to tell the world I just wanted everything to be all right. Still, everyone from doctors to milk-mothers to vile-fathers, even my own thoughts disregarded the storm clouds.

There were storms and violent clashes that filled my brain like titans, forever at war in my head. I built pantheons and prisons endlessly and erroneously where geometries didn't matter nor the price of reason to hold them up. As I grew older the storms grew worse, clouds growing ever darker over a horizon that I'd never reach when all the complex-partial what-ifs laughed in my face. The rest of the world didn't understand and saw only my blank stares and their questions unanswered decayed like I'd secretly enjoyed them squirming at all the possibilities.

I had millions of them.

I wanted to scream, but the storms were always so fucking loud, beating ceaselessly against the shores and cities that filled the dusty reality that was my head.

They grew worse too—the storms, I mean. Sometimes I forget things, and how people cast their gaze on me as if something was wrong with me, especially when words break down in my mouth like wet crumbs, pieces of rock and ruin. Falling out of the pan, not to temperature, smashed against the counter when I knew everything was bent and bruised on the inside, but there was no way to put it back together. And yet,

the storm was brewing

along the horizons.

The inside storms.

Still, the milk-mothers, vile-fathers, the pantheon-places passed their judgments over me when I couldn't understand and thought me a stranger, foreign and bizarre. The insular worlds where cities and Cyber Gods, as terrifying as they may have been, were the only places where I felt solace, or reasons despite such abject horror.

I always dreamed in cities, places that were unimaginable outside the storms and stares. Temples that climbed as high and vast as the stars themselves and friends so outré they cared not for my condition, but my company alone.

You're back, they'd say. Stringy and cryptic I recalled their voices, which never felt like voices at all, but whispers from some memory or desperate recall.

It's the only place I can come back to, you know—before the Storms, I'd say while I saw their face, silver without eyes, only wide silver teeth grinning from edge to edge.

"I know. The storms are getting worse, aren't they? It's dangerous coming here, you know that, right?" The Silver Thing had a name at one point, but it was irrelevant. To me, he was the only friend who understood me.

I kicked my feet and avoided their smile. "I know, but there's no point attempting to get anyone else to understand. It's as if my stomach is filled with a gnawing, awful familiar sensation. I know the storm is coming and it's going to be worse than the last."

"If that's true you can't stay here. You know what happened the last time." The Silver Thing's grin began to fade.

I stood on the shores of an infinite mind, my own, at the base of a pantheon built from my dark comforts. "I don't want to leave this place. *They* won't understand this time. Things are only getting worse out there. They don't get me. It's all symptoms and psychosomatics with them."

A bony mass of shadow cracked, pointing towards the sea. "Do you see that?"

My stomach was heavy. The skies were thick with a conversant danger where lightning began to crack the skies and the clouds fomented with a sinister hunger.

"You can't stay here," they said. "You know what will happen, don't you?"

I wanted to ignore them and carry on like so many times before. A crack of thunder tore across the sky, lightheadedness filled me. "The storm will swallow it all. You, the shore, the temple. Everything. Then I'll come back, and we'll do this all over again. So what?"

"Not if you don't leave," they mused, most sternly.

All at once I was dreadfully fatigued, but there wasn't a sense of urgency to flee, to leave the dream only to come back and be surrounded by a sea of unwanted eyes. The endless prescriptions that never offered relief, but a continuum of cause and side effects.

I never knew the true nature of the Silver Thing's face. Its eyes remained shrouded conspicuously behind my glassy thoughts and the webbed darkness of clouds and laughter. But I found comfort in never knowing their true face because they were the one person or thing, who never judged me. Never saw me for anything except a bundled mass of neurons and atoms.

No, I didn't want to leave them, but I had no choice.

"I suppose I can't outrun the storm, can I?"

The toothy silver grin returned. "Perhaps not, but you certainly can survive it, and you will. Besides, you won't always need me, and I won't always be here when the storm clouds gather or when there are people who don't believe you."

It was time, like clockwork, I failed to prevent yet another storm which attempted to press me further into oblivion.

Perhaps the same creatures I saw in my head, the tempests which sabotaged my ability

    to think,

        to scream,

            to tell the world

I just wanted everything to be allright.

The words *petit mal, epileptic* were no longer signifiers to haunt me and fill me with a sense of derisiveness, but rather they remained; becoming like a scar which never healed. Always and forever, a memory of blank stares and absent storms for when the clouds gathered.

They were right, my friends. I never saw them again, in dream or nightmare, there was no sign of that toothy smile, or cryptic tone rolling over the shoreline. So, alone, I waited, standing on the beaches of my mind where I feared the day when a black fog rolled across the horizon I'd never reach.

And . . . so I wonder, when. I wonder . . .

Hallucinations

I remembered this place. These visions
like high walls coalesced into a fortress,
I'd traveled here, once before,
through the wild strands of dream or death;

long before cities were scattered
across the earth like some irksome locus,
before enough was enough.

Always there persisted,
in the abysm of my thoughts,
helpless flecks of me,

crawling in the fever-pits,
wishing to get out. The last bones
and broken objectivity of hope.

Pathetic and cruel were these subjectivities
understood to me as the *all-possibilities,*
and the nightmares of a species

never meant to reach this point. The point
of something beautiful and dreadful,
an imagination curdled by blood and one hundred million years.

How did I reach this point?
The feeble construction of me,

floating, drinking, breathing,
texisting in the improbability
that was the randomness of existence
—beaten like rubber;

amazed at my own grotesque resiliency,
and also wondering at the day
when the fibers would be too weak
to hang on for another pathetic moment.

Nothing could explain the architecture,
the wild symmetry of towers
and finger-like spires along

tunnel networks of my otherwise
brain-bled reality whose haptic-betrayals
jockeyed my beleaguered soul, back and forth, without rest;

I begged someone, somewhere,
in the webs of my tired consciousness,
a reason for this tiresome opera;

played over and over again;
its heinous music bashed
through my skull until I knew nothing
else except its monotonous words, *enough is enough.*

Soon I was tossed back into the Wastelands
of rotted memories where the black dreams
of race covered in flesh

with hearts of metal,
birthed that which was most monstrous,
the Cyber Gods.

These were the first beings who lingered
within the darkest thoughts and bleakest
philosophies before the stars themselves

found their molten sparks,
and no cities or matter,
but black dreams. Before enoughs

were swallowed by nameless tomorrows
or yesterdays and somedays smashed
by the machinations of the new gods of the present.

Though, in the beginning, I thought
there were no gods, beasts, or stars.
Only the mute darkness which

remained unsettled; no before-thens
or after-somedays. I recalled them
as brief flashes of light as if

some bizarre nostalgia infected
my thoughts; pixilated mirrors
reflecting the crimson madness in my head.

Click. Tube-machines and milk-mothers
gave me the first glimpse of a world-to-come,
where the night was replaced

by computer-stars and suddenly,
there were no more flesh-selves like me.

Click. Wait, there was more.
Wrought by the bleakness of my own invention,
through the darkest portals of unshaped light

and reason there came the first *things*
who stepped out from a nameless pantheon;
intent to mold us, commentate and cure the universe

No,

       that's

              not

                    right.

There were gods in the beginning,
I made them, but these *things* were different.
They weren't like the other ones.

Stringy and malignant, I watched them
through reason, or perhaps hallucinations,
as I'd always understood them to exist;

fourteen billion years in the past,
they writhed in splendor.

When the *Cyber Things* established
their countenance o'er an unending night,
it had then become their

stringy bond over the universe,
bent to their atomic will.

Entrenched beneath sticky mounds of dream-bile
and gray-matter,
I saw manifested plastics of the future.

History and myth blurred
into sparkling forgetfulness
where hallucinations bled through my consciousness,
over and over as endless cycles of bile and blood.

A Place Called Nowhere

In a cabin at the end of the worst,
most unimaginable parts of
my desolate nightmares without
climate, or uncontrollable
something-storms and blundering,
empty words like Raven-songs,
there was a place called Nowhere

Wild, unwilling and mad, were the fields of cruelty
here, at the midway point between the blessed and baleful,
a purgatory of my own design in a place called Nowhere

Deep, pushed into the membranous turf
that was my brain, without direction and somehow
I found this place called Nowhere

when
without fail,
when,

when there wasn't
                enough of me left
when so little made sense, pushed around
    by self-made, self-proclaimed tyrants, standing on bones without brains,
        who saw themselves as saints

when they were but murderers
and maniacs, refusing
to understand their actions or insipid presumptions, all while
bloated planetoids imploded
when stars collapsed
around them, and me,
coalesced into a closet
which became my self-made refuge;
when storms grew worse with every thunderclap
and lightning bolt scarring the night sky,
and Syntax became nothing
but syrup and sick-suckered words, used to
corrupt my already misshapen cortex
with mini-nightmares
when the closet door no longer latched, and the nightmares
followed me to places that I thought were sanctuary,
and I felt like there was no way out, or back home
when the waxed burned to its base and I couldn't handle the
darkness any longer,
when so much began to dissolve into the shadow

in a cabin at the end my worst,
most unimaginable parts of
my desolate nightmares without
climate, or uncontrollable urges,
when things actually began to make sense again
and I saw there was a place called Nowhere
when syntax transmogrified by ridiculous,

darksome spontaneity twisting the midway point between the blessed and
    baleful;
when words I *thought* I'd seen, spoken, or heard
       came back as if to guide me, or rather incircle me in a purgatory of
my own design
when a place called Nowhere lost every aspect of dimension and
             reason,

when
without fail,
when,

I found this place called Nowhere

Cycles over Cycles, If Only

Cycles

    over

        Cycles, meaninglessly, the continuous processes of the someday which played through my head as if they were pictures without a story, characters without purpose;

        Cycles of shapes that destroyed each other over and over again until there were no more shapes, only colors and vile words, betrayals of syntax;

        Cycles like monsters who enjoyed the pleasures of pulling down deeper into mechanical clutches where fingers twisted into;

        Cycles of meaningless enoughs and somedays until I could no longer bleed, never understanding that enough was enough, watching my flesh-self shrivel up;

        Cycling endlessly pulling me towards the cold fires of silence, scarring me, over and over in a black and white film that never stopped playing;

        Cycling abusively until there were no more screams left for me to drink or tears to bathe in;

        Only cycles, endless, repetitive motions like the spirit-bile vomited from my dreams never ceasing as the tube-machines piped more and more brain-funk through;

                        Cycles

                    Over

                Cycles.

Tube-machines cut towards the beginning of everything, where something else knocked on the other side of my worst nightmares. A time where tube-machines and Cyber Things plagued me not but existed as a fantasy in the wastelands of my imagination.
I remembered when songs were always enough,
their music so sweet and gentle,
and nothing more was required of me.

No expectations for the future.
The words at the end of each sentence were like crumbs or an aftertaste from the sweetest cake, baked only for me.

Flesh-self,

imagination,

Cyber Gods, black dreams,

the present, head, me, the universe,

splendor, atomic will, purpose, syntax.

They were only words, nothing more.
And I thought nothing of it.
Not even the gods or forces
that inspired them,
only that nothing was required of me,
and I felt as if I had existed within some heavenly bubble stuck out of time itself.
Wait, it's happening again, I think.
Movement from one side to the other in a place without walls, or reason.
Yes,
that's
right.

There was nothing before this, even if I felt at peace within this construct, idea, whatever the fuck it was.

The tubes were endless, like everything I imagined, built with bile from sour brain-matter, and the liquescence of my yesterday; I was told, no, made to thank my machine-mothers whose charitable programming gave me the curse of questions without answers, processes without fulfillment, someday without a desire for self-destruction; the need to worship material gods without means; the emptiness of tomorrow without the full present belly; the damnation of *cycles* without end;

And the dreadful music that once was so beautifully twisted through rusty tubes as songs of enough clogged my ears in an awful repetition.

Lovely things, ugly things, trinkets and bones, translucent clusters coalesced into a mass-like thing;

Lovely bodies, ugly bodies composed with slime-star matter, whose perfumes cut my nostrils and as of the bloody reminders weren't enough and;

Lovely thoughts, ugly thoughts, wildly coaxed my seemingly haunted brain, drunk on the possibilities beyond my bedroom window;

Lovely dreams, ugly dreams every night like some virus, a cold without cure that sieged my brain with visions of crimson poppy fields, marble spires, and whispers beyond far canyons whose

Lovely places, ugly spaces weighed on my ability to think or *want* to think on the possibility that those hallucinations might be anything else except,

Lovely tubes, ugly tube-places winding seemingly endless through a corroded and brain-bloodied world that used to be my imagination like roots bereft of water and sustenance,

Yes,

That's

Right.

If only there were enough songs to be sung when the days ended in cacophonous wailings and;

If only the appointments drawn up to the stars were good enough for me, for the people who swallowed their beauty every night;

If only the lights produced by hellish forges, unreachable by death could provide enough warmth for the coldest hearts;

If only they wanted less than adequate, confiding within the plastic coffins of tomorrow-when, something shiny and green;

If only there weren't cities to clog the skies or bleed the earth, or scratch the bellies of elder things;

If only, then there'd be some end to the endless, dreams worth remembering or pictures whose art that scarred the mind's eye;

If only I dreamed in cities, no longer, but places without metal or man, or Cyber Gods, curse-less, stripped of banal cruelties, and;

If only the Plastics understood the terror of their replication, where by every cultured pixilation led simply to another useless light;

If only there were no more tube-machines, or dumps for spirit-bile to fill my mind with virtual excrement like some place-bin of nothingness, until the next batch is ready;

If only I wasn't ready. I am not ready for that nameless, awful tomorrow, that which stands on the other side of someday, howling the primal screams of never-again and only-when;

If only I might stay in this place, trapped in the cycles never-ending, consumed in songs of enough never to step across the threshold of tomorrow;

If only, but choices weren't guaranteed, only disillusioned and gray as if staring into a mirror, the chiral madness like some grave joke where the laughter crashed against my body and the only shape I saw, was that nameless tomorrow . . . if only.

The Gates of Nowhere

Deep in the pit-nethers of Tomorrow,
I saw loneliness and cold
all around me, withered voices

and body-branches crunched
like deadwood-dreams. A piece

out of time, crystalized and strange,
along the waters edge caught my eye;
a howl, a broken mirror with

my shattered self, a scream for tomorrow
and I began my descent towards
the ruins of an inferno all my own.

Always in the void, so far do
these things begin, and
so often they end

within the places cut out of shadow,
death, and despair. I
spoke in quiet whispers

at the edge of a familiar
place, Nowhere at the
border of Oblivion whose gardens

where shown to me by visions
wild, and episodic like violent storms.
"Come, here we make the descent

here, beast, monster, and gods
merge into something new
and desperate, and familiar."

Came an ancient voice,
the Father of Poets:
"When, without fail,

we're summoned to return
to the Gates of Nowhere,
there's no turning back

except for the Fall,
whereupon through every ring,
every demented terrain,

all meaning, sense, and purpose
swirled in euphoric disillusion."
I followed him, without any choice, along the deadwood path where my eyes
were lifted to the Castle Someday;

where the tired exuberance that
was a brilliant and belabored horizon,
dragged towards infinity,

I saw the terrible Castle Someday. High and proud
was its architecture with towers

hewn from marble, granite, and bones
of desperate, lonely men,

who thought themselves masters
of the inevitable, and inscrutable structures
which climbed inexorably towards the unsettling skies;

whose stars danced above as if to taunt
the onlookers that something was coming.
Bloated apertures gave caution

for those who dared to enter
the Castle where crooked mirrors,
rusty pieces of ancient armor

from a nameless forgotten civilization
lined the old carpets along a series of
demented Gaudian corridors, which weaved

in and out like some grotesque,
labyrinthian queasiness. The scent
of metal and burnt wax filled

the stone halls mixing with a
viridescent spectral glow. There were few,
who knew the truth of the Castle Someday, and its

dreadful existence. Deep inside, secrets of the impossibility of stars swirled
within pits far below, languishing in chains long since

thought to have perished to Time's lugubrious song.

Concealed in the strangest, most unsettling basements beneath the dust and derisive thoughts

which pressed o'er the endless ages
as if fat and heinous digits; prepared to asphyxiate a single voice—the last possibility

twitched in silent shadows,
calling from a crooked dungeon,
I am the end.

The last note,
a string pulled in the lowly dark
whereupon its soft and lonely tone hung in the deep,

sad recesses of the night—*I am the end.*
Concealed no longer, the foundations
of that ancient castle gave way,

jubilantly, to its immutable destruction
where the tired exuberance that was
a brilliant and belabored horizon,

crumbled against infinity,
and I saw at the end of everything,
the terrible Castle Someday.

And yet, I knew, I was neither at the end,
nor close to anything that might be called the beginning;
and long after my time was done,

expectations left me to linger in this world,
the last of some forgotten thought,
or race discarded; fatherless, faithless,

passed over by Devils and Gods and Mirrors
I was cursed to watch and wait
beneath the nethers of the world in dank, shadowy caves;

A bastard from a nameless line,
contrived in flesh, and clinging to billions of candles
dripping with pearls of wax and poor decisions,

each lip curdled until the flames were extinguished one after the other and
relit as if new sunsets might suddenly be birthed by maniacal, ancient forces;

I was cursed to watch and wait,
long after my time was done,
left here, when, without fail,
The forgotten, Someday.

Where the end begins,
begins the end. Trapped
in awful chirality, straddling

the reflection of myself
in a world I never understood.
The burgeoning weight,

From the New Century was too great,
like a ball of iron pressed
against a cotton sheet, it was

only a matter of time
before the fibers snapped and
my synapses dissipated into

the vapors of a new, unforgiving age.
Gods, I prayed for the day things broke,
or when everything shattered and I fell

towards that mouth of mirrors below,
the reflection of a billion Nowheres,
their gates unreachable, except within my broken thoughts,

When I attempted to pen these dreams
of a foggy nothingness as if to leave myself a key

when
without fail,
when,

never mind;

Never mind, was where
the end begins,
begins the end.

Loathsome machinations of my own broken imagination seemed to be the
only constant in a world that was filled with disappointment, hatred, and
false promises.

　　Maybe one day, *they* might understand me?

　　　　Maybe

　　　　　　one

　　　　　　　　day.

the days were getting shorter, tempers thinning and my ability to stare into a dreamless, faceless space was growing ever so intoxicating.

Towards the crumbling edge of a hungering abyss,
I saw that which was monstrous;
swirling oceans of ink, blood,

and phlegm congealed with thick
foaming waves of rust and bone. There,
a mouth of mirrors, swallowing dismembered closets

and hopeless souls like me
into an unholy maelstrom of sequestered norms
and white oblivion, where light and love

were nothing but craggy what-ifs
drowning below the crimson, inky waters.
The thrashing waters were sharp,

cruel reminders of a terrible music
beating in the distance,
trapped between the darkness of choice.

I'd seen this all before,
heard these sounds,
tasted these putrid waters,

Lingering in the aromatic stink of the night,
a song reprised from the darkest parts of my mind,
a city that never was, haunted

by neon queens gliding over deserts of broken bottles,

placated by their whiny torch-songs
dancing in the tired dead streets.

This city, built on the margins
of my rattled brain,
its foundations planted in scar-tissue

and syntax as its signifiers
bled through my eyes like broken windows.
These were the shades of dead rainbows,

wandering aimlessly in this modern Asphodel,
pushing others and those like me into that gaping abysm or sucking us
completely of worth and dignity—

when
without fail,
when,

never mind;

Never mind, was where
the end begins,
begins the end, and

    Maybe one day, they might understand me,
      Maybe
          one
            day.

                I'd have more time,
              or a choice for that matter.

Since when did we have a choice?

Plagued by my own thoughts as a parade of old,
ghostly queens prodded at me
through derision and costumed tatters
draped so elegantly over gaunt, twinky skeletons;

I'd have more time,
or a choice for that matter.
Since when did we have a choice?

Behind me, below me,
I was trapped,
between the darkness of choice;

caught betwixt the mascara and macabre
of a city of dead rainbows and the gluttonous,

darksome waters below. All at once,
slops of syrupy ooze coughed
onto the edge of the cliff,

where liquescent droplets of glass
collected at my feet as if salivating for my flesh,
never entirely sated. Never did I,

Nor anyone presume to understand how the world came to this,
the scent of moldy, bleached skin engendered by the night,
pressing my senses with heavy, bleak perfumes.

No, this wasn't the life I wanted, straddling two worlds,
 never fitting into either one but, continuously being forced to pick one.

"You made your choices," protesting I stepped back from the cliff,

turning up towards the jagged towers of cracked skulls
dripping with diamonds and death while tattered shadows and ashy caftans
waved like a scabbard, fallen from a sunken ghost ship.

> I thought I'd have more time,
> or a choice for that matter.
> *Since when did we have a choice?*

The words, the structures fell apart as if the dream itself began to lose its shape and substance and nothing else made any sense including the Mirrored Ghouls who sought my desperate retreat.

They wanted nothing to do with me, or my words—only the taste of a boy whose reflection was still fresh in the glint of awful mirrors. They were impossibly different, dressed in rhinestones and tears, the shine of their garb matriculated with bizarre reflections of the yawning abysm in front of me. My body reacting in the most profane ways imaginable, excretions of light and fluid unnaturally spilling though my ears. Time was running out, ticking away as the queens of black, brown, pink, and yellow stars tried to flee the dying city, hoping for one more taste, one more bite.

No! Come back! Come back to us, decrepit fingers, polished with blood and silk reached from the glittering dark beseeching me, but there was nothing for me here. I saw their hideous, androgynous forms collecting at the Void of Other, smashed together in a tiny room flung towards bottom of the universe's distended belly like a mouth of mirrors.

Their desperation grew more ravenous, thirsty, filled with a plutonian urgency as a thunderous cloud of oxidized horror barreled through the cluttered alleyways, toppling buildings, and ripping apart already broken streets tossing silky, caftan covered bodies into the air.

I saw them, racing towards me with craven eyes, ink pooling into the wrinkles whose existence they'd deny, but there was no time. Trapped between dead rainbows and a mouth of mirrors, I had no choice. *I never had a choice.*

Suddenly, my body was tense, swelling with a numbing paresthesia, like needles in my skin when billowing plumes of iridescent bodies piled in a shimmering mound against me, the old queens pressing me closer to the edge, their profane torch-songs crying in my ears and the lustful mouth of mirrors below. Towards the edge of a hungering abyss, I saw that which was monstrous; swirling oceans of ink, blood, and phlegm congealed with thick foaming waves of rust and bone.

Through the Gates

i. Canto Prologue
No! get off me! Please, I'm not ready to go!
I protested the cold sheets flung off my breast,
Another night cast into oblivion.

A crooked empire long gone, one forged in silence,
with ruins scattered in the undulating dark
at the feet of the pantheon; where puppets and corpses

littered the streets under dripping, cracked towers.
Towers of my creation, worlds hewn
from the stone of my throbbing imaginative viscera.

Colossal were the shadows swaying
in light of a heavy dawn as the pallid derma of my thin frame
reacted to the warm particulates of the immature, yellow star.

"What am I even doing?" I rubbed the sleep from my eyes.
Wandering in fields of literary garbage, worms, cosmic untruths,
and towers built of beautiful poetry;

I'd no reason to believe I belonged in this place,
whatever it was. A wasteland of withered imagination.
There was an empty notebook by my bedside with a simple title
etched in smeared ink, *The Pantheon.* "One day, I'll finish it."

the smell of fresh roasted coffee drew me towards the light.
Someone was downstairs, dressed in shorts, a baggy shirt
draped finely over an impressive athletic physique

plastered across their chest. We'd been together for over a year now,
and life was *fine*. Everything was always *fine*.
Though there were many days I spent more in inside my dreams than reality.

It was safer there, safer than being a *Yellow Star* or *Broken Rainbow*
here in world that never wanted me in the first place.
Needless to say, maybe was looking for something inside my dreams,

desperately attempting to piece together something stalking me
a story that wasn't even my own;
the truth of gods beyond the pale of reason.

I should write all this down someday,
though the Pantheon upstairs remains: empty. I mused.
I had seen the Gates of Nowhere, passed through them even once before.

Always without subjectivity, or substance,
only meaningless words splattered
onto a page like discarded open cans of paint.

Repressive deduction without art, wrinkling the skin,
sucking away those beautiful ghosts. Still, it was hard
to discern dreams from reality. The touch or taste

of what was or what could-be as my body trembled,
my feet pressed into a warm bluish gold sand,
the smoothness of the particulates against my skin was sensational,

despite experiencing this countless times.
"You might as well enjoy it while it lasts,"
came a soft whisper from atop one of the sandy dunes.

"Not you again," the light reflected off the sand.
I knew this voice. My familiar guardian, "What do you want with me, now?
Have you not plagued me enough? The sun is almost up

and I'm no closer than I was the night before to reaching the end.
Or the night before that, or the night before
that one in this hellish place I call my dreams." Without a second thought,

the proximal of my fingers contorted with pain
as blue sand poured over them, "but what's the point?
Always in my head, and never outside.

It's not as if this night would be different from any other night,
or like I'll be able to discern what is or isn't.
That the sands might simply disappear

into oblivion at the peripherals of my eyes
leaving crystals of salt and memory for me to wipe away
until I'm left with another doom to repeat, over and over again!"

The anthropomorphic philosopher-gargoyle stretched their wings,
the stone and iron cracked as two faces
protruded from a neck of fungi and moss.

"We are here to guide you," one of the mouths twisted.
"Doubt, and delirium, two halves of the same whole," the other head
looked at me as if to mock my disposition in this place

And continued, "these lands are composed by your dreams, not ours.
And will follow you down towards the cradle
of those terrible gnashing thoughts in the Pantheon of your dreams."

Adorno and Horkheimer, Delirium, and Doubt
were my two consistent friends in this *place,*
away from the repression that was reality.

I watched while the winged-philosopher beast
stretched its crippled wings, the raspy voice
like crinkled leaves coughed in the wind,

a broken saucer in their claw, "take a sip. It soothes the nerves."
Adorno chortled, a piece of their wing cracking off,
"And you know they can't actually drink this, so what's the point?

If not for the destruction of truth, where into the mouth of reason
a great fury waits at a place confounding reason.
Waiting to swallow us all."

The Pantheon, at the bottom of the world, through the Gates of Nowhere
where dreams were pressed into crumbs and atoms,
pathetic and forgotten until lost in an oblivion of unreason

I knew what awaited me here. The same story every night
for as long as I could remember,
and the story was always the same.

"Sure, if that's what you want to call it. It's your head, not ours.
Thoughts aren't scared here in this place, either,"
Horkheimer bemoaned while drinking the nothingness of the air.

ii. Canto Pantheon

Myths were built and bled from the bones of my tired neurons
like roots unable to seek moisture, unable to dig deeper
where in the coldness of this frozen existence,

the hand of enlightenment throttled me. Away from the world
that doubted me, eroding my mythology of *Something*
whose syntax constricted my being.

I watched my guardian slowly disappeared into the darkness.
I stood at the gates of a place confounding reason,
The Pantheon whose genesis I'd pondered almost insipidly
was a massive temple and mausolean structure,

this monument to my oblivion. The anthropomorphic Horkheimer-Adorno
stretched their wings of stone and faces covered in fungi
peered down at me as I approached the alien palace.

"Carry onwards for destruction of truth,
into the mouth of reason and find the fury that rests
at the center of the universe,"

my two-headed guardian whispered as the Pantheon
loomed higher it's craggy features
sneered like broken teeth.

Delirium and Doubt / Horkheimer and Adorno
stepped away from the light of the sun
creeping over the cliffs

A new transition,

something falling towards

the center of the universe,

iii. Canto Nath'Zrath

my descent continued, and there were others too in this place,

others who sang these familiar songs.

Dawn crept along the horizon

still hesitant to make its entrance. The predictable

melody began like a classical overture,

strings bowing and the grin, growing to an awful crescendo

until I'd see a terrible smile plastered across the skies.

Trembling under my skin, a frightened pragmatist

danced under a storm of needles, preparing to cut me down.

Uncertain, unwilling to justify the false truths

seeping through my rotted pores,

I was left with blood and myths.

Across courtyard crawling along marshes of gold and mud,

where rusty tracks zigzagged like some kinky discordant up melody,

twisting itself into nothing but atoms I crossed the threshold.

Truth was a matter of opinion here. Stepping

into the wide cracked rotunda where stars

themselves seemed unphased

by the ruined physics of my dreams,

I watched as the demented tracks of Nath'Zrath warp and bend,

the metallic warbling pounding

against my ears as if I were being
asphyxiated by sheets of aluminum foil.
Oxidized snowflakes coated the ground,

the metal-snake train god awoken,
rubbing brittle calcite and rust from *Its* eyes,
bemoaning some mournful yawn.

From fangs made of screws and a tongue of plastic,
syrupy words spilled over me.
Who are you? What do you seek in this ruined place?

My mouth was covered,
unable to speak so as not to inhale the poisonous stench.
Blood poured from my nose,
To finish the story. To finish this damnable song.

The metal-snake train god licked its rusty fangs.
Train tracks rumbled in chorus
with their gods displeasure.

And what song is that? One that seeks to consume you
and this beleaguered universe,
created by your own pathetic machinations,
where your soul finds itself trapped,

begging for some pathetic release
that might never come? Who are you to ask for such a release,
to hope the song will end for you, or for any of us?

The hardened bits of aluminum, gold, and bone liquified
until they formed a cast around my feet,
leaving me at the will of that hideous titan and I remained silent.

Answer me! Fool! Do you not wish to see this truth
and all probable truths crumble without considering consequences
even if for one moment the pale,
tired existence dared to end without any care for

those who'd follow you to this place?
Swallowed into the nexus of oblivion, the dark recklessness
will follow you for as long as the Void knows silence.

Silence remained my crown as I hung my head beneath
the toxic god as the metallic chains melted away
and Nath'Zrath bowed *its* head in the open rotunda,
the cloud of toxic smoke dissipating around me.

iv. Canto Gulaplast
Above me, the sun began to close in with rays like solar swords
meant to cut deep inside more than some stellar corpse.
Even the stars who found themselves

swirling in the vastness around me
twinkling with dreadful worry
until they were nothing but dim torches.

Failed atoms that were never enough

There was little time left.
I pressed onward, deeper into the Pantheon,

corridors transmogrified into eye sockets,

panels danced and columns twisted as if they were never

made from stone to begin with;

and the rotunda finally crumbled into ash,

the pitiful moans of that metal-snake train god

wailed in my ears like a wounded dog. New images

and old ghosts with old pillars carved

from carved basalt and ivory, seawater and glassy sands

teased my nostrils. Below, mossy cliffs

and leafless dead shrubs dipped

into an endless expanse of ocean;

raging and writhing under a tenebrous sky.

"Why have you come here?" came a thunderous clap,

covered by the lapping oceans yet masked with bellicose growl.

I knew it was a beast so great and terrible,

the oceans were unable to conceal its monstrous wrath.

I looked over the cliff into the vast ocean where

three great amber eyes brightened underneath the waves,

"Same as I told the snake god."

"Then what do you wish to find here,

that you couldn't find elsewhere or

through the council of The Great Nath-Zrath."

"The ending," I cried, "I just want it all to end.

I'm tired of *this night* where nothing makes sense

that enough never seems to be enough

where I can't even finish my own thoughts
as they deteriorate right before my eyes.
Even my own syntax and signifiers

fall apart as if to confound my journey.
Each night I try to piece them back to string together
some coherencies, but nothing."

Falling to my knees on the cliff, all at once,
hundreds of tentacled arms burst from the uneasy waters,
Gulaplast's amber eyes dilating with fury,

"Yet you've come here, to me, every night.
To this place, a pantheon within your destroyed mind.
A desolate schism in both thought and polluted philosophy,

for our counsel; and only the spectres
which seek to illuminate your fears a
re that you'll never be *enough*.

That the stars might burn bright in infinity
when in truth they will die.
That this will collapse over and over again,"

the Great Gulaplast with words of thunder, terror, and salt
bubbled up from the seas,
continued their remonstrate,

"You watch us wither and die in your mind
as the sun rises every morning,
knowing full well you'll simply return every time

you come rest with Oblivion
to ask the same useless questions. The same prattle,
when even the Cyber Gods have become slave

to your dreamy exile. Wandering in fields of literary garbage,
worms, cosmic untruths, and towers built of beautiful poetry.
Where do you think this Pantheon came from?"

Tears rolled down my cheeks,
the heat of the sun touched my back.
Those solar swards were close and the destruction of truth,

my rueful admission to this illusion gone awry.
Disenchanted, I was left to commiserate with a bleak reality.
Gulaplast released me and sunk back into the depths of the sea,

fleeing to from the wretched flames of the sun, but to no avail.
The waters quickly turned to steam leaving the immense deity
exposed to the deadly rays, a bloated carapace rotting under the radiating heat.

"Wait! Please, come back," I cried as the great monster disappeared.
A body that may have never been,
beached on the shores in a world entirely composed of my own delusions.

Soon I found myself lying in a scorched desert of megalithic corpses
filled with snake-gods, train tracks,
and fish things piling onto one another only to become forgotten relics
in my subconscious, burnt by the sun and my mind.

v. Canto Zot

Spastic, dazed, and unnerved I awoke
surrounded by the Glass and Hours
whose desert belonged to no one,

not even me, paralyzed
by the cruel antics of mysterious
forces at edge of the horizon.

"Why doesn't this look familiar? Where am I?
I've never visited this place in my dreams.
Do I still find myself in the Pantheon?"

"Keep going," a whisper called across the Glass desert. said.
"What? Who said that?" I called out.
"Zot," It called.
"Zot?" I repeated.
"Zot . . . Zot . . ." the voice chanted.

"What trickery plagues me so?
Show yourself as either phantom or god,
whatever you are! Where are you leading me?"

Time. It beckons for us all here,
can you not see the sun is almost upon me and still, I
have no way to end this terrible music

which presses against my brain like stone
upon the brittleness of flesh and bone.
Oh! Delirium! You vengeful, false guide

promised me the truth,

but now I see only darkness and the inevitability of Tomorrow

as it haunts my every step.

Despite reliving whatever this was, night after night,

somehow there were moments that I couldn't recall,

as if my mind pushed them down into this place.

Away from me, away from everything.

"Follow Zot . . . Zot. Zot wishes you to follow.

Zot speaks truth to the untrue.

Zot knows what is or isn't

or that Cyber Gods can or cannot be

without *this place*. Zot knows.

Zot has always been and will always stay,

here, with you. Follow Zot . . . Zot wishes you to follow.

A voice dripping with wires and syrup,

I found it familiar and strangely comforting

though there was no form to it.

The Glass and Hours went on and on,

leaving the light of the sun nearly at dusk behind us,

but still there as a warning it'd come for me.

The distant glimmer remained, growing and dimming

again and again as if it were a different form of star,

while the sun I knew had all but disappeared.

"Zot?" Nothing.

I'd only heard slippery whispers in the desert winds

cutting across the dunes as I waited for a voice that never answered.

"Answer me! What is happening. How can it get so cold in this place? Zot?

Are we almost there? Zot? I am following you!"

"Follow Zot . . . Zot. Zot wishes you to follow.

Zot speaks truth to the untrue.

Zot knows what is or isn't

or that Cyber Gods can or cannot be

without *this place*. Zot knows.

Zot has always been and will always stay,

here, with you. Follow Zot . . . Zot wishes you to follow.

The voice of Zot faded

until there was nothing left to follow,

nothing to hear except the silence in the dark.

vi. Canto Hazthrog

Completely surrounded in the dark, the glimmer of light resting on an unknown horizon, I meandered towards it.

My teeth chattered as the crushing gloom of night weighed on me. "Zot likes to come and go," said a voice, speaking as if made entirely of the whispering air.

"How can one take sickness in a dream? Feel coldness and tiresome worry when things are not even real?"

The air rushed from the northern edge of the desert and the voice grew colder, "Who says one cannot meet Death or Sickness within such a place? That these dimensions are none other than gateways to one's own Oblivion? Isn't that what you've begged for every night?"

"What? I never meant for this," Coughing, I looked around unable to discern any visible figures in the night.

"Who said that?"

"I did. Most know me as Hunger, Plague, Contempt, but my true name is Hazthrog. Seems you've *caught* me in the damning cool of the night and like the *others* I too will succumb to your *erratic* and feeble consciousness."

Suddenly high above me, a green shelf cloud began to erupt with waves of lightning and thunder followed by a low bass cackle rattling the sandy ground below me, "Have you figured it out yet?"

Flashes of light and scratches against the night, like some ancient static rattled my brain, "I—I don't," coughing and struggling to breathe I saw cracks in the shelf, eyes or something. "I—can't. I can't, my lungs. The story—I am close—I think," heaving slightly.

"You're close. Try not to waste too much time on it though, there's little of it left," Hazthrog said.

"But the light," I tried to speak.

"Yes," the old god whispered as if attempting to comfort me, its miasmic tongue curling around my body thrusting me across the desert, "You're close to the end."

"Same as every night?" I said, feeling a little dizzy from a lack of oxygen.

"More or less. It's better just to say that you're close to the end," it whispered as I watched the shelf cloud begin to disappear, the lightning wither into atoms and the viral Hazthrog dissipate like some Hadean shade retreating across the River of the Dead. There it was, the light of the sun quickly spreading across the desert as if Hazthrog's cloud was holding it back.

vii. Canto Ad' Naigon

"There it is, the star," I sighed, looking ahead to the glimmer of strange light I was journeying toward. Physically, I don't know how it was possible, but I was exhausted. I managed to cross the desert; however, the viral god had done a severe number on me.

"I made it—this has to be the end," pleading to some nameless thing, the exhaustion becoming too great for me, my face drenched in tears. There, wide steps leading towards a stone portico with crumbling pillars on either side supporting a triangular pediment with gruesome iconography carved into the center of the structure.

The approaching sun pushed me underneath the pediment where I was met with a familiar amber glow. The radiant burst swallowing my body as I laid my eyes onto a swirling mass of stars, planetoids, and galactic bodies floating inside the rotunda of the pantheon. A different rotunda, possibly. Above, they all converged towards a single source, a globular molten ball belching with wild entropy, heat, and coolness. The Nuclear God, encapsulated by an immense liquescence of silver, gold, and metallic rock swayed in the vacuousness of space. And I realized that I had been here before.

"I've been here before," I said, looking into the infiniteness above and below, a bleak and sudden terror washing over me, "I remember now."

I remember the face of Ad'Naigon perched on a throne of ivory, whereupon one billion dead races lay buried; the temple that led me to a place inside my dreams and story I saw, finally coming to conclusion. There was no way to describe the Nuclear God's voice, only that audible burst rupturing my ears, blood and bile dripping down my head pleading the last few words crawling from my lips, "So you know what comes next? Do you remember, how this story ends? Please, someone, anyone take this nightmare away from me. I can't handle the uncertainty anymore."

All at once, the brightness of the morning weighed over me as the pantheon began to collapse, column over column, bricks and bone tumbling into nothingness. Rubbing the sleep from my eyes, and ruined pieces of that forgotten pantheon, I looked toward my nightstand where unfinished manuscripts and some dried ink pens sat as the morning sun bled through my curtains.

Sitting up, I felt dried tears staining my cheeks, hands trembling afraid to touch or even look at myself. One of those beautiful ghosts, fated to relive some Sisyphean doom, over and over again.

"What am I even doing, anymore?" I said, disenchanted, wrought with frayed visions of my fragile mythology, prepared to shatter into tiny bits of oblivion tomorrow night.

Someday and the King of Loops and Cycles

In cycles over cycles,

I desperately longed to find,

So much more than what I thought I would be,

buried in

graveyards of stars

A promise by someone

their word as worthless as

their body

which was nothing more

than platitudes in syntax,

taunts to my tired soul, and too often I found myself drawn back to a moment, a time where I knew something as tender as flesh, or cherished as love and somehow it all was revealed in shadow as atoms, beneath myth and mania—

Someday—that inevitable prophecy, love Me, Someday.

I desperately longed to find the graveyards of stars. We all knew that stars died, collapsing onto themselves with unimaginable weight and incalculable devastation.

They were the resting place of gods, whose wide, full tombs like mouths stuffed with the dirt, treasure, and worms from places that never were and always had been. They were the Gates to Someday, the window to the other side, a key to the mysteries that Death kept so close to his chest.

The greedy bastard.

I was so hungry to find the graveyards I'd do anything, befriend any demon, or take any chance. It's been said that any place were stained by death's touch no matter who or what were fixed points. Gateways to that endless nether place where cities built in gold, blood, and stars were wrapped in night and Death himself, conceals his greatest treasures from those who'd wish to steal it.

No one wanted it more than I did.

"You've got to die to find them. To find *him.*" That was according to my so-called friend and self-proclaimed ecclesiastical sycophant, Dionysus Bolt.

It wasn't important how we met as much as he was sickly intrigued with the graveyards as me.

I'd looked all over the New Ashworth metro area which had its share of publicly run cemeteries and apart from the demented folklore, I didn't really know what I was looking for, apart from Dionysus' cryptic, and silly clues.

"The graveyards. They are the way points. That's how we find the Gates to Someday," he'd say sometimes in a zombified daze, after having too many energy drinks. He smoked a lot and I found myself too, somewhat attracted to his almost religious zeal.

We'd crept through every reasonable boneyard and dared to breach the walls of a few private cemeteries as well, but at the end of the night we found nothing but dull, quiet statues and lingering fog.

Finally, one night, Dionysus suggested the old grave of St. Cyr near the Maumee River Bridge. According to many, and him, mostly him, the bastard child of a god died here, forsaken by his cosmic roots the creature was left to die and many claimed to have seen the light of a dead child, the cries of a forgotten calling out to the stars.

"The many who died here were said to have been shown the path to where the Gates of Someday lead. So, maybe this'll be the place we can find it. Babe, wouldn't that be amazing if we actually found it here?"

Amazing, yeah, of course. I wanted this, right? I mused to myself. *Why wouldn't I want this?*

Dionysus pulled my arm as we approached the watery limestone path near the drop off next to the bridge.

"Are you sure this is the place?"

"Yes! I knew we should have searched here first...I don't know what you were thinking," he said.

It wasn't worth the argument, and even if I tried, Dionysus always had an answer for everything. "You're right, let's just get this over with. I'm just starting to get tired of this. Maybe there's no such thing as *Someday."*

Dionysus sneered, his hunger for the truth was as strong as mine, but my resolve couldn't match him. He stood there, a long, youthful countenance outlined by the yellow glint of the moonlight.

"This was your bleeding fantasy. I only wanted to help you find what was on the other side. And here we found it, together."

He took my hand, grasped, well, completely enclosed it; so, there was another piece to our relationship I forgot to mention. Love, graveyards, and the search for death. Nothing was ever black and white, but as long as Dionysus was there, I knew things were going to be alright. Besides, it's hard to search for Death's Door without someone who *really* understands you.

Dionysus never led me astray, at least not on purpose. I couldn't back out now, especially when his eyes appeared so otherworldly, their milky glow reflecting off the ancient statues in the St. Cyr graveyard. Strange things attracted me to men, but old legends, and stone guardians ticked all my boxes.

"Are you all right, now?" He continued, still holding my hand.

"I think so. I'm sorry, I think I'm just scared that we may actually find what we're looking for out here."

Admittedly, I was terrified.

The name *St. Cyr's Gate* was plastered in rusted, metal letters across the entryway where black bars wilted under the weight of so many centuries. Gargoyles crumbled by the day, their bodies barely able to hold their own stony bulk, and misshaped headstones littered the dying grass patches as we, well I, nervously trudged through the cemetery. Dionysus on the other hand was as giddy as giddy could get. He, for lack of a better description, dragged me along. The anticipation built up inside my head was so exhilarating, but finally standing here, I felt as frozen as one of those statues.

The winds were soft and unsettling as they gowned the area in dust and quiet darkness.

"Dion," I called him sometimes, "What exactly are we looking for? Does anyone even know what the *Gate of Someday looks* like?"

He ignored me, flashing a whimsical smirk to ease my cautionary attitude. Soon, that charming visage melted away, expressionless, our hands together, his eyes were fixed on something, but I didn't know what. The moon was high over the graveyard, and I felt a disconcerting, almost nausea growing in my stomach.

He said you have to die to find it, I thought to myself. *He was joking right? He doesn't really mean . . .* My pace began to slow, unconsciously, not paying attention until a heavy tug pulled me to the ground and my mouth was filled with dirt and worms. The smell of blood flooded my nostrils and for a moment, I'd swear on everything that was reasonable, I saw something. The lights went out as if my eyes were sealed off and there was nothing but electric neon and a gateway.

Time was irrelevant, swirling deeper inside my throbbing brain was an endless tomb of stars. Falling and rising as if an ocean of liquid infinity, real and unreal, spiraling deeper towards some inconceivable center. Someday was mine. Finally, it belongs to me and no one else. I didn't even know if tears were possible where or when I was, but I never wanted to leave.

All at once, I was throttled from my infinite pleasure where all the stars left my wide peripherals replaced by sky, grass, and stone. Tears were soon real, blood became substantial, and smells were a contemptible jinx that tickled my neurons, over and over again.

"No . . . No . . . I want to go back." I pleaded in a hushed breadth while Dion stood above me.

"Are you all right?"

"I——I'm fine, but where . . . where am I? What happened?" Babble and useless phrases were all I could muster right now, because I only wanted to go back, back to Someday.

Dionysus kneeled, more concerned than I'd ever seen him before, "You fell, babe. I'm sorry. I got too excited, and I must've dragged you as we were walking, and you hit your head on one of the headstones."

My fingers were stained with blood and my head was cool and warm at the same time.

"Where did I fall?" The world was tumbling, but I only wanted to focus on one thing.

Dionysus pointed toward a nameless stone. Many were old families, broken plots, and forgotten people.

"You were right," I said matter-of-factly.

"What?" Dion looked puzzled.

"I was there." I stared blankly into Dionysus' eyes. "Don't you understand? I found it! Him, whatever."

"What do you mean? You——you hit your head, babe," Dion said.

"That's not important! You were right. Everything we talked about. Remember? You have to die to find *him*. To find Someday. I found him. I don't know exactly what, but I found him, Dion.

"Whatever you did, you have to do it again. It was beautiful, I saw everything. The stars, the gateway to Someday. The cities. It's all real."

My bloody hands grasped him; Dion's long arms coiled feeling the still warm blood stain his skin. The realization was too much, but my hunger and gait returned when I finally spied the great, unendingness where everything was nothing and nothing bled from the spirals of tomorrow.

"Babe, you need to see a doctor, that's what *we* need to do. Let me carry you or you can lean on my shoulder, and we can get out of here, alright? Maybe you were right, and this went a little too far."

"No!" Blood began to drip down my forehead. "I know what I saw, Dion! This is what we've been trying to find, for god knows how long. We've searched the whole fucking city. Everywhere! And look, we found it! Now you want to back out? Sorry, I can't do that.

"You've no fuckin' idea what I've seen. I saw stars die and reborn. I saw all possible futures and *his* throne. If you love me, for us, you'll do this. And whatever you did, I need you to do it to me again. Or else I'll find my own way back to *Someday.*"

Dion stepped away visibly shaken by my grotesquery, and for once, I was proud that my resolve *finally* outmatched him.

"You can't ask me to do this to you. If you love me, you can't ask me to do this," Dion pleaded.

My concentration was beginning to wane, perhaps the loss of blood or the adrenaline pumping through my body, it was fuzzy now. Everything was fuzzy, unclear, shapes and places grew into shadows of whatever they once were, but I tried to remain centered on Dion's voice.

"Babe? Can you hear me?"

Yes, every word, but on the other side of him I saw the light of someday, flickering like a torch beacon across a galactic ocean. All the sudden, it was as if I were floating in an ocean of sludge and stars, paddling for an oar where Dion's hand reached for me on some unreachable shore; and on the other side Someday called, "Swim for the lights."

"Yes, give me your hand," Dion pleaded, although I heard the tears in his voice I didn't want to reach out.

The other side begged me to wade through the bog of shimmering blackness, and I knew what awaited me.

"I'm coming, I promise."

My voice was barely audible, I thought at this point. The scent of blood grew less and less to me, but more and more to Dion. Soon, fading into something nebulous and vague, but the heavy embrace of familiar sensations, a gentle hand, old cologne, and last regrets were enough for me to hear Dion, one last time.

"I'm right here, babe. I'm sorry, please don't go like this. Just hang on for a few more minutes, okay? I've called 9-1-1 and they'll be here soon. And when we get through this, we'll never come back to this place, or any graveyards again, okay?"

I wanted to acknowledge him, to let him know he was right and that we'd put this wild, cosmic adventure in some cobwebbed coffin and bury it;

but I couldn't do that. I'd gazed upon something indescribably wonderful, and shedding my corporeal existence was worth every what-if.

I did hear sirens, but by that point it was too late. I desperately longed to find the graveyards of stars, the Gateway to Someday and I found them. I found that which was unattainable in life and promised in death.

Dion never let go, but through the last audible whispers I had to tell him as we sat in the old graveyard, sirens mixing in the silence of a thousand years, "Love me, Someday."

i.
Dion Lied.

I found that they were here, and I followed Someday, through the columns into the Place called Nowhere, and I found Love and Death, Someday was mine, trapped forever in cycles over cycles in this song that never quite had an end; a Sisyphean tragedy whereupon my tired and haggard soul was pulled across rusted barbs and rock-bones of the Earth, a place I thought I knew.

A world that I thought held promise for me and those that were mine, searching for treasures that became as useless as my body and brain and yet, I begged the Cyber Gods to end this manufactured mythology, a spoon-fed tale of my life that never really held promise except for the wild, darkness ahead of me.

ii.
And soon, I knew the Cyber Gods were dead. Streets were filled with a new voice, terrible and wild as the people cried, *The Cyber Gods were dead;* and without a precious second thought, or worry, I saw the pallid, crusty ivory faces, which waited in the muck and misery rose in song to the chorus of a

new and horrific age marshaled by the parade of familiar voice who sang—
The Cyber Gods were dead.

And while the streets cracked, the white faces screamed into the fading horizon ever so confident at their decisive slaughter, and I wondered if the Cyber Gods *were* really dead; and despite it all, the ire of the White Faces never ebbed, never waned, and never was enough even though the *Cyber Gods were dead,* but enough would never truly be enough—even for the White Faced King of Loops—

Proem Reprise

Loops cursed infinitely, some caught in a broken cycle—over and over—visions of what was-to-come, the terrible chorus in my heart like awful ides continued their tempo when enough was enough and truly, it never was enough; again, inside a city of skulls, displaced and falling backwards, upwards through a spiral towards that which was always broken. A song that played over and over again until my brain bled, and even that wasn't enough.

You're almost there . . .

Almost, where the ghosts of my own

❀

Infinite and Alone

Everything before now, existed as hallucinations wrought by instruments of cyanide and dreams; where palaces built along phantom valleys, connected by tissue and tarns, swayed against the yawning horizon of silence. Replicating cities and spirit graveyards bubbling with bile and bone, I walked through the dirt-ridden landscape toward that time-place without a name, shapeless and old.

You're almost there. I'd hear familiar voices creep into my head, familiar songs and cycles playing over and over. Until at which point, I reached a tower. A boring, simple structure whose bricks were extraordinary, powdery white and cream. Stretching high above the other buildings I was pulled to its dreary façade. Through a pair of crippled doors, I was blasted with the songs of enough cruelly repetitive machinations whose machinations never knew the sweet comfort of resolution.

I was almost there.

Tomorrow within my grasp,

And I'd had Enough . . .

Never and finite were the dumpsters of wasteful minutiae, piled high toward the fleshy, vaulted ceilings that were my head. *Enough of the shit,* I said, but I found myself covered in it, tissued tingly nothingness without meaning but still thrived for a pitiful ounce of signified reason.

I thought, no, thinking is wrong, in this place. I found I was in a different place. Perhaps the City of Skulls was never real to begin with, but some simulated vomit of consciousness. There were streets that snaked across boulevards where dead things that might have been trees or flowers, wilting against the stone pots, beseeched me; their hungry pores wishing for one last drop of something. The thirst for something new.

Steel towers like skeletons from a bygone age, stripped of flesh-metal, were laid bare for the world to see them for what they really were: meals for progress.

Finally, alone, the music was gone whereupon my eyes touched the graveyards of Cycles and Silence, endlessly stretched toward some rusty, burnt horizon. My lips caressed the

bones of tomorrow while the flimsy structures that attempted to cut the night were torn down, throttled by heinous shadows. Never had I been so heavy, lonely, and free while Time's mushroomed girth pretended to asphyxiate me; compel my choices;

Finally, the stars were going out and the machines turned to rust. Each ember, down to the crippling molecular tower, falling to their own machinations and;

Finally, I'd no longer dream in cities or societies; plastic races hellbent to bathe in shit and false philosophies, but cleansed of the spirit-bile that leaked from my head;

Finally, the tube-machines were ripped from their flesh-sockets and vile-makers thrown into the same vats of smiling mechanical instinct, where;

Finally, the last screams bled from my lungs so painfully, everything dry and tired the last bits of anger and hatred seemingly dissipated from my body and;

Finally, there was emptiness, chasmed by the ugly strings of wiry shit and a mundane putrescence;

Finally, I was done, collapsed under the weight of the nameless tomorrow, free from the conservative fuckery that was me, us, or them. Shapes consolidated into light and legends, dispatched into the atomic source code of will-be-so and;

Finally, nothing mothered, infinitely so, even the most basic primal cyber-clamps were shut off, and there were no more songs, or enough-saids, simply finite breaths;

Finally inhaling the last few bytes of pitiful molecular rations, promised but never guaranteed when;

Finally, I screamed again, my body dried wholly of spirit and ink wishing for an awful, swift end, but no relief ever came; merely the haunting kiss of silence that said;

Finally,

    you

        are

            alone . . .

inside a closet of stars.

Here in this place,
a Closet of Stars smashed against
the breast of the universe;

where I was locked away. Deep
in the blackest, insolent
moments of history.

I saw the Castles of What-if

and the Palaces of Not-enough
crumble like forgotten songs,

dusty and ancient, and still,
there was never enough.
No words to speak, or questions

to answer from the darkest
corners of my mind
where only dark closets

as dim and dull
like dying stars waited for the
cycles to restart. To burn

the wretched scars of memory,
deep, unfathomably deep
into my brain. To switch

on the tube-machines
again and starve
the milk-mothers and vile makers.

Finally,
      I

          was

              alone . . .

inside

a closet of stars . . .

if only . . .

If only I'd never hear those words again, to be free from the closet and chains under the blackest skies and darkest nights whose sweet melodies of oblivion offered me deathful comfort in the wake of such stupendous and awesome loneliness;

If only I hadn't looked up to see the stars concealed by cellar doors, trapped behind my own eyes and confounded by the bleakest lies constricting my soul, making each day heavier than the last, every breath so precious;

If only the cyber-beasts pressed their fingers over my body again, blasting this abhorrence of reality through my skull, but how did I get back here again? Trapped in cycles over cycles;

If only there was a way out of this place, where doors were stars and the night hung by the nape of a rusty hinge on the Gates of Someday, ready to snap, like me;

If only the god-things and vile-makers knew what they created, but I watched the stars go out, the lights dim, and the doors shut, leaving me trapped inside this swirling refuse of haughty judgements, false gods, and white hooded daemons;

If only there was a way to stop it, never and finite were the anguishes of tomorrow, always barreling towards something that would never end but the heaviness of it all . . .

The heavy

    Door of Stars

  Swung

             toward tomorrow . . .

Enough Is Enough

And there, at the opening of the end, I cried, enough is enough when Cataclysm married Reason to birth something endlessly grotesque, though unbearably enduring and the songs trumpeted across that which <u>was</u> and never-would-be at the same time when enough was enough; the end smiled, and I was prepared to cut its throat as mutilated syntax and tongues salivated over silicone corpses;

Who thought they'd reached the end, the last cycle, but too late as their journeys were in vain when they saw the horizon unreachable and the Cyber Things laughed;

Who knew the truth, the darksome, twisted logic that nothing was as it seems, and enough was the song we'd all find ourselves doomed to know, scratching at the backs of our minds were cycles over somedays bled in metal and fluid;

Who decried the fucked-up platitudes where monsters howled against the backdrop of Boomers and Bile, clamoring and conspiring to breed false promises;

Who never understood, but coated themselves in the needless cyclical slaughters, the Plastics deserved everything;

Who put their children in concentration, housed in the name of freedom, fed the fodder and lies with microwaved shit;

Who deserved more than enough, placed by the visions of someday and starless nights that climbed deep beyond the eyes of gods;

Who saw nothing, visionless, blind, and cold in the darkness of space they were relegated to a fate worse than death, but idealization;

Who built the corpulence of banal things, meaningless ideas, derived into simple constructs as dead pieces of light and laughter;

Who tickled my darkest nightmares with that singular fucked-up

    question,

        relentlessly,

            incessantly,

                enough is enough.

If only . . .

                                Yes,

                          that's

                    right

I've been

            here before, inside

Cycles

    Over

    Cycles, somedays where the gates were too wide to shut and the days processed in tube-machines that fed virtual milk and marrow through the tunnels of tomorrow; connected into slot-brains and bone-sockets when;

Cycles over somedays were replaced with what-if-then's that played over and again, the endless dreams as if the cinematic platitudes attempted to convey anything but the truth and;

Cycles bleeding against the backdrop of blistered *why-me's* tarnished my simulations, the perfect lie that someday would arrive and the fucked-up life-flotsam cleared away while

Cyclical monsters birthed again from their tube-masters and vile-demons as the corpses of milk-mothers lay dried and empty, the cycles ready to start over and over again beneath the towers of a New City, the Plastics kneeled, submitted to the Cyber Gods that thought themselves their masters when;

Someday, the awesome repetitive ideal, puppeteer and god-thing snickered from behind a veil of stars at their inane and silly machinations, but I'd seen these hallucinations in the beginning when nothing was everything and stars were like blood spots on my skin;

And Someday destroyed the City Skulls, again and again reconstructing the hallucinations where enough was never enough and my body weightless o'er the deadness of tomorrow waiting to repeat

Cycles

Over

Someday

When the End

Was truly enough.

Not Since Extinction's Prayer

Not since the Twentieth Day had I witnessed so much destruction, unnecessary and endless, when the skies turned black, and fires mushroomed from plumes of white fire, the blasts of banal rhetoric jettisoned by their sovereign hosts blanketed the world in a desolate, deathful beauty and;

Not since I'd watched through stereophonics and pixilation, the talking heads crying into the void, "the sky is falling," those in metallic cities who disregard their warnings, heads in the sand and eyes promised to metal-devils;

Not since the days where buildings crumbled like old bones, so dusty and brittle, and the heat of tomorrow was too great, too hot for the people of yesterday to bear witness and I felt my body melt away in the intensity of that awful someday that burnt my precious eyes, skin, and pathetic body;

Not since the world was comprised, computerized, and boxed up for the me to use on payment and pride with the false pretense that its resources were anything but mine, belonging only to the privileged mass who hungered for the last crumbs;

Not since the days where the Marble City cracked and its ivory columns foundered while the powdered ideologies cemented in partisan blocks, flimsy and laughable, tumbled to the landfill-homes and lavatory-palaces leaving us in decay;

Not since the fields turned the ash, the trees withered to hollow barrels like the corpses of yesterday and the souls who dragged themselves through the foggy death-lights, beseeched the vile-makers and tube-mothers that they might feed the planet-children, giving them life;

Not since the dirt-bodies and spirit-bile were drunk by wild metallic beasts, leaving only barren and bone to cover that endless, endless night, and;

Not since the day when I saw the first hairless, flesh-things crawl without words sputtering through their lips *progress becomes me,* until soon swords became their teeth and plastic their blood, and gold, their only food, then, did I regret everything,

at

the Bottom

of the World.

My Fingers
at the Bottom of the World

At

the Bottom

of the World my fingers were lost in the desperation of muscle memory, gliding across the bright screen, haphazardly searching for something unknown to me. Perhaps the missing byte within the vastness of the throbbing cyberdark, or another crumb for my tired eyes to swallow. Through viridescent pillars where scrum-lords and winged things, augmented by a new reality connected by data points and dogmatic deserts, the future was near.

Toward the bottom of the screen, the world was trapped in the uselessness of signified places whose words and places were ignited by mythical identities as we traveled deeper, farther down towards the bottom to a place where eyes could not see, but the mind was pulled, placated, and plastered.

Thrown against the tissue-wall of the influencer, the laughter from above pouring down the tube-machine coating my brain and body in the hallucinations and hatred of pixelated gods as if to taunt me in all the possibilities that never could be, but only as close as we wanted it to be, scrolling faster and faster with the awful truth we'd never reach

the bottom of the world

inside the belly

of fat, cyber things, who controlled

My fingers scrolling faster past the flash-moments of our day,

with fire, war, and love as if they never existed in the first place, but imaginary
constellations within a universe I'd never truly understand;

My fingers waving across a bright screen whose faces were never
mine, but the nameless friends, ghosts, and demons that haunted my
nightmares and filled my dreams each night;

My fingers which ached, calloused by the endless swipes to the left, to the
right, up and down, reacting to the blasted by the rhetoric which burned
those great cities whose high towers I'd never seen, only in the fuzzy images
behind screens and synapses;

My fingers broken and blunted by the heavy-handed thrusts of tech-dread
which pushed us farther and without any sense of stopping until we bled,
baked, and watched forests ignite in fiery clouds of ash and laughter; all
within the false protection of screens and banshees pulling;

With fingers and phantoms faster into the deep, cyber underbelly of
tomorrow who cared not for the pathetic flesh-sacs, never-borns, and helpless
neophytes that paddled in the rising waters of the present unaware the future
was ready to collapse at any minute;

My fingers which trembled, desperate to reach the bottom as if salvation there was an answer to save us all, to save me from the impending uncertainty that barreled towards us without any care;

My fingers!

God damnit,

when will I—will we

reach the bottom,

or was the world

truly bottomless?

The screens were as bright as the Songs of Silence whose Cycles bled over and over again within my mind, but enough was enough!

I'd been here before, inside the dark-down-deep and I saw the darkest pieces of us, broken, lonely, and exposed for Tomorrow.

To Swallow
the Deep-Down-Dark

Deeper, through the treacherous parts of myself, past the jagged ramparts where doubt pressed hard against my skull;

Deeper inside the corpse of my estranged imagination whose blackened dreams charred the landscape as if stuffed in the belly of Hell;

Deeper where no one cares, but only enough is enough and that damned music plays on and on, to pull me one step closer in a world I'd never see;

Deeper into the bottomless, thankless night where the stars went out all over again and I was strangled by tube-machines, and plastic-sons who ridiculed me for having everything, yet they, nothing;

Deeper, deeper, were they lost in the world and so, too, was I the Cyber Bastard without name who swiped neither to the left or right, but forward and fell;

Deeper into another cycle over cycles, infinite and alone to realize that enough isn't enough, but it's all that I have, though I craved more;

Deeper, into the far-down-dark scratching, clawing through the webbed mess of names, places, and falsified hopes and unlisted realities there had to be something else;

Deeper, hidden underneath the signified bastardizations that mocked me, over and under every pathetic piece of myself . . .

No More Absent Storms

There were millions of them,

Millions of words,

Millions of dreams,

Millions of storms,

and they surrounded me with their infinite,

electrified breath and bile.

Silent dreams and strange signifiers that reminded me of the palaces and pantheons whose designs I might never know, or even in my wildest nightmares dare claim to understand. Roaming deserts of glass and bone stretched in all directions while lightning bodies danced above in purpled heavens, begging me to return to a place that might destroy me.

"We told you not to come back," a familiar, dark whisper called through the tongues of night. The only friend I knew in the cold, frozen endlessness.

Fat clouds billowed in the distance, their groaning thunder was enough to tell me things had changed since my last visit.

"I had to come back," my feet sank deeper into the glassy sand, blood and debris covered my skin.

There was nothing to come back to, no temples, or pantheon-places, only decayed, gaunt bodies of the vile-fathers and milk-mothers who had become the sand and subdued by the fat, depressing weight of time.

Finally, the rest of the world understood and saw my blank stares and their questions unanswered decayed like I'd secretly enjoyed them squirming at all the possibilities.

Perhaps the creatures I saw in my head, the tempests which sabotaged my ability

      to think,

           to scream,

            to tell the world

I just wanted everything to be alright knowing why I returned; that I might scream words like *petit mal, epileptic, broken, mine,* and the storms for the first time, were calm.

Fifteenth Cycle

Enough

When I finally found myself screaming enough was enough, my body throttled back towards the beginning of an endless cycle over cycle;

When I was again wrapped in the idealized nothingness of a tomorrow that might never come and,

When I was repeating the same songs, eating the same tasteless words, forgetting parts of myself in the shadows of a distant world that never was,

When I prostrated myself at the feet of a faceless beast in desperate hope to be recognized that enough might finally be enough,

When I found myself weak, stripped of any voice crowned by silence and metal thorns all the while, Old Stars grew heavy and hungry,

When I begged for the songs to stop and enough to truly, be enough and the song that played ceaselessly the music of spirit-bile again and over with deathful charm, and;

When the trumpeting to cosmic drumbeats, those new gods, the Cyber Gods birthed from senseless thems and others, the reprise that brought me back despite my resistance;

When things like a pleasurable burst of stars and strokes; were the not beginning of humanity's unraveling spiral towards that which remained, but my ruin, a broken city of skulls, displaced and;

When the hunger and inclinations continued, which were never enough I screamed towards the Old Stars, where tears were impossible;

When those silent wishes and meager protestations meant nothing in the face of absent storms that grew powerful and angry, continually in the deep;

When the gates collapsed and the hordes rushed in, no one suspected anything, in fact they welcomed it;

When the teleprompter-paladins failed to halt, but empowered the hordes who sucked them dry and left the world dazed and dried up;

When the cable-body castles were razed and left to rot in wiry boneyards for a careless future with influence gods who stood on loudspeaker shoulders

When the new order came to be, the Cyber Gods were dead, and the hallucinations meant nothing but were craved as if they could mean everything to tell everything that something else meant more than the blood on their hands

When the world collapsed while columns of flames reached for the skies and even the stars began their retreat;

When Dream Tyrants crossed over into reality, our walls unable to hold them back, our towers to small;

When their siege engines destroyed everything and nothing made sense we longed for a Pantheon to call our own, or a Nowhere without justification;

When hallucinations were everything and nothing;

When enough was enough and I'd do anything to beat the songs beyond silence and the visions of what-was-to-come;

When through my most desperate proliferations, enough was *enough* I sang those words with utter intensity, the loop broken.

Proem Finale

Enough was enough when the music ceased and the drumbeats ceased and the gods halted their inane chatter in ruined halls amid cloudless skies; without fearful worship or repetitive pedantic mythologies regurgitated over and again through a bloated and broken universe that was never truly enough for them, or me. And while the hapless and tired realities crumbled around me without reason I embraced finally, with the solemn heaviness that enough was enough and songs and the songs that sought to continue their tempo like awful tides in my heart, the terrible chorus of what-was-to-come, a vision—over and over—a cycle *truly* and forever broken—freed me from this infinite cursed loop.

www.ingramcontent.com/pod-product-compliance
Lightning Source LLC
Chambersburg PA
CBHW071149090426
42736CB00012B/2276